GATEWAY TO JOY

GATEWAY TO JOY

Reflections that Draw Us Nearer to God

ELISABETH ELLIOT

VINE
BOOKS

SERVANT PUBLICATIONS
ANN ARBOR, MICHIGAN

GATEWAY TO JOY

Vine Books is an imprint of Servant Publications especially designed to serve evangelical Christians.

Published by Servant Publications in conjunction with *Gateway To Joy*, a ministry of Back to the Bible.
Servant Publications
P.O. Box 8617
Ann Arbor, Michigan 48107

Editor: Evelyn Bence, with assistance from Mindy Wilson and Laura Goodspeed
Illustrations: cover, pages 24, 37, 64, 76, 106, 117 © Charles Neal / Superstock. Used by permission.
                 pages 12, 47, 81, 95 by Claude Monet from Planet Art.

98 99 00 01 10 9 8 7 6 5 4 3 2 1

Printed in the United States of America

ISBN 1-56955-121-9

LIBRARY OF CONGRESS CATALOGING-IN-PUBLICATION DATA

Elliot, Elisabeth.
    Gateway to joy / Elisabeth Elliot.
        p.   cm.
    Includes bibliographical references.
    ISBN 1-56955-121-9 (Servant bookstore ed. : alk. paper). —ISBN 1-56955-122-7 (GTJ deluxe ed. : alk. paper).
    1. Meditations.   I. Title.
BV4801.E63   1998
242—dc21   98-27287
                                                                    CIP

Preface

Joy, said C.S. Lewis, is the serious business of heaven. The business of earth seems often to load us down with disappointment and sorrow. Where is the joy?

It has been only in the last couple of decades that I have, to my astonishment, discovered that every experience, even the most unwelcome, if offered to Jesus, can become a gateway to joy.

Through overwhelming loss the prophet Habakkuk learned the great lesson of *choosing* joy. He said, "Though the fig tree does not bud and there are no grapes on the vines, though the olive crop fails and the fields produce no food, though there are no sheep in the pen and no cattle in the stalls, yet I will rejoice in the Lord, I will be joyful in God my Savior" (Habakkuk 3:17, 18). This was a deliberate act, not of the emotions, but of the will.

Suffering and joy are closely linked in Scripture. When Jesus was preparing His disciples for His departure He reminded them of His obedience to His Father. He promised them that they too, if obedient, would remain in that same everlasting love. He said, "I have told you this so that my *joy* may be in you and that your *joy* may be complete....You will grieve, but your grief will turn to joy."

It is my hope that as you read the following selections, five for each letter of the alphabet, you will find the truth of His promise.

Many thanks

to Evelyn Bence, who served as the compiling editor for this book.

She was assisted by Mindy Wilson and Laura Goodspeed.

ACCEPT ...

The Sunshine of His Face

When I was fourteen or so I began to think seriously about the words to one of my favorite hymns, "Beneath the Cross of Jesus."... Was I willing to accept only *the sunshine of Christ's face (when I could think of all kinds of "sunshine" I hope for), to "know no gain or loss" (I had several ambitions)?*

I wanted to be willing. It was going to take some learning.

A Path Through Suffering

Beneath the cross of Jesus I fain would take my stand,
The shadow of a mighty rock within a weary land;
A home within the wilderness, a rest upon the way,
From the burning of the noontide heat, and the burden of the day.

I take, O Cross, thy shadow for my abiding place.
I ask no other sunshine than the sunshine of His face,
Content to let the world go by, to know no gain or loss,
My sinful self, my only shame; my glory all the Cross.

Elizabeth Clephane

ACCEPT ...

To Find Peace

He said, "I will forget the dying faces;
The empty places,
They shall be filled again.
O voices moaning deep within me, cease."
But vain the word; vain, vain:
Not in forgetting lieth peace.

He said, "I will crowd action upon action,
The strife of faction
Shall stir me and sustain;
O tears that drown the fire of manhood,
    cease."
But vain the word; vain, vain:
Not in endeavor lieth peace.

He said, "I will withdraw me and be quiet,
Why meddle in life's riot?
Shut be my door to pain.
Desire, thou dost befool me, thou shalt
    cease."
But vain the word; vain, vain:
Not in aloofness lieth peace.

He said, "I will submit; I am defeated.
God hath depleted
My life of its rich gain.
O futile murmurings, why will ye not
    cease?"
But vain the word; vain, vain:
Not in submission lieth peace.

He said, "I will accept the breaking sorrow
Which God tomorrow
Will to His son explain."
Then did the turmoil deep within him cease.
Not vain the word, not vain;
For in acceptance lieth peace.

Amy Carmichael,
"In Acceptance Lieth Peace"

Accept

WHATEVER BEFALLS

This, then, is of faith, that everything, the very least, or what seems to us great, every change of the seasons, everything which touches us in mind, body, or estate, whether brought about through this outward senseless nature, or by the will of man, good or bad, is overruled to each of us by the all-holy and all-loving will of God. Whatever befalls us, however it befalls us, we must receive as the will of God. If it befalls us through man's negligence, or ill-will, or anger, still it is, in even the least circumstance, to *us* the will of God. For if the least thing could happen to us without God's permission it would be something out of God's control. God's providence or His love would not be what they are. Almighty God Himself would not be the same God; not the God whom we believe, adore, and love.

Edward B. Pusey

Taste and see that the Lord is good.

PSALM 34:8

9

ACCEPT ...

God's Place for Me

Lord, I would clasp Thy hand in mine,
Nor ever murmur nor repine;
Content, whatever lot I see,
Since 'tis my God that leadeth me.

Joseph Gilmore

O what a happy soul I am!
Although I cannot see.
I am resolved that in this world
Contented I will be.
How many blessings I enjoy
That other people don't.
To weep and sigh because I'm blind,
I cannot, and I won't.

Fanny Crosby, age eight

BLESS ...

This Day

Loving Lord and heavenly Father, I offer up today all that I am, all that I have, all that I do, and all that I suffer, to be Yours today and Yours forever. Give me grace, Lord, to do all that I know of Your holy will. Purify my heart, sanctify my thinking, correct my desires. Teach me, in all of today's work and trouble and joy, to respond with honest praise, simple trust, and instant obedience, that my life may be in truth a living sacrifice, by the power of Your Holy Spirit and in the name of Your Son Jesus Christ, my Master and my all. Amen.

The Lord bless you and keep you;
the Lord make his face shine upon you
and be gracious to you.

NUMBERS 6:24-25

Bless . . .
MY SLEEP

My Lord, my Love, my heart's eternal Light,
Shine on Thy lover, through the hours of night.
Shine on my thoughts, my very dreams be found
About Thy business on some holy ground.

Should friendly angel come to meet me there,
Let me not miss him, deaf and unaware.
And if I may, one other prayer I bring,
O Lord my God, make no long tarrying.

Amy Carmichael,
"Before Sleep"

BLESS ...

These Guests

Sleep sweetly in this quiet room,
O thou whoe'er thou art,
and let no mournful yesterdays
disturb thy peaceful heart.
Nor let tomorrow scare thy rest
with thoughts of coming ill.
Thy Maker is thy changeless friend,
His love surrounds thee still.
Forget thyself and all the world,
put out each feverish light;
the stars are watching overhead.
Sleep sweetly, then, good-night.

From a wall plaque in our family vacation home,
Franconia, New Hampshire

Bless
THIS MARRIAGE

O God, you have so consecrated the covenant of marriage that in it is represented the spiritual unity between Christ and his Church: Send therefore your blessing upon these your servants, that they may so love, honor, and cherish each other in faithfulness and patience, in wisdom and true godliness, that their home may be a haven of blessing and peace; through Jesus Christ our Lord, who lives and reigns with you and the Holy Spirit, one God, now and for ever, Amen.

The Book of Common Prayer

BLESS ...

This Birthday

What I want to wish you today is joy. I want you to have the happiest birthday ever. Not because you're just exactly the age you've always dreamed of being: the perfect age. Not because you'll be having the splashiest, roaringest party ever, or because you're surrounded by all your favorite fans, feeling marvelous, getting a vast pile of gorgeous gifts. I could merely wish you a happy birthday, but I'll do more than that. I'll turn my wish into prayer, and ask the Lord to give you the happiest birthday ever. I'll ask Him for the kind of joy that isn't dependent on how you feel or who's there to celebrate or what's happening....

I pray for you on your birthday, that your path, as is promised to the just man, will shine not less and less but more and more; that you will still bring forth fruit in old age; that the Lord will give you a thankful heart....

So—happy birthday! If you have friends and parties and presents, be thankful for such bonuses. If you have no friends with you today, no party, not a package to open, you still have a long list of things to thank God for, things that matter much more. A birthday filled with thanksgiving and hope is the happiest kind of birthday. Have one of those! Deck yourself with joy!

On Asking God Why

COMMIT ...

To Whom? For Whom?

A story is told of Jesus and His disciples walking one day along a stony road. Jesus asked each of them to choose a stone to carry for Him. John, it is said, chose a large one while Peter chose the smallest. Jesus led them then to the top of a mountain and commanded that the stones be made bread. Each disciple, by this time tired and hungry, was allowed to eat the bread he held in his hand, but of course Peter's was not sufficient to satisfy his hunger. John gave him some of his.

Some time later Jesus again asked the disciples to pick up a stone to carry. This time Peter chose the largest of all. Taking them to a river, Jesus told them to cast the stones into the water. They did so, but looked at one another in bewilderment.

"For whom," asked Jesus, "did you carry the stone?"

These Strange Ashes

COMMIT ...

My Life

Take my life, and let it be consecrated, Lord, to Thee;
Take my hands, and let them move
At the impulse of Thy love.

Take my feet, and let them be swift and beautiful for Thee;
Take my voice, and let me sing
Always, only, for my King.

Take my silver and my gold, not a mite would I withhold;
Take my moments and my days,
Let them flow in ceaseless praise.

Take my will and make it Thine, it shall be no longer mine;
Take my heart, it is Thine own,
It shall be Thy royal throne.

Frances Ridley Havergal

COMMIT ...

To Service

*T*here has often been a tendency to think of service to God as necessarily entailing physical hardship and sacrifice. Although this is not really a scriptural idea, it has gained wide acceptance. It is easy to recall the saints who climbed the steep ascent of heaven through peril, toil, and pain, but the Bible also makes mention of Dorcas, whose service to God was the making of coats....

When I lived in the Auca settlement ... some [correspondents] envied me, some pitied me. Some admired, some criticized. I could not help asking myself if perhaps I had been mistaken. Was I really obeying God, or had I merely obeyed some misguided impulse, some lust for distinction, some masochistic urge to bury myself in the forsaken place? There was no way of being sure what was in the murky reaches of my subconscious, but I was sure I had committed myself to God for His service, and I knew no other motivation. The opinions of others—whether they commended or condemned—could not alter my duty, but their very diversity caused me to ponder carefully what that duty was....

My duty was one thing, theirs another. My responsibility lay here, but the responsibility of some of my correspondents who gazed starry-eyed at my role lay perhaps in an office or a kitchen or the cockpit of an airplane.

The Liberty of Obedience

Commit

AT ANY COST

When I was sixteen years old, I copied in the back of my Bible a prayer of missionary Betty Scott Stam's, whose visit in our home when I was very small had made such a deep impression on me. Her prayer:

Lord, I give up all my own plans and purposes, all my own desires and hopes, and accept Thy will for my life. I give myself, my life, my all, utterly to Thee to be Thine forever. Fill me and seal me with Thy Holy Spirit. Use me as Thou wilt, send me where Thou wilt, work out Thy whole will in my life at any cost, now and forever.

The cost, for her, was quite literally her life only a few years after she had prayed that prayer. (Betty was martyred in China in 1934.)

These Strange Ashes

Constrained by Love

O Love that wilt not let me go,
I rest my weary soul in Thee;
I give Thee back the life I owe,
That in Thine ocean depths its flow
May richer, fuller be.

O Light that followest all my way,
I yield my flickering torch to Thee;
My heart restores its borrowed ray,
That in Thy sunshine's blaze its day
May brighter, fairer, be.

O Cross that liftest up my head,
I dare not ask to fly from thee;
I lay in dust life's glory dead,
And from the ground there blossoms red
Life that shall endless be.

George Matheson

DESIRE ...

Fixed Where Joy Is Found

Almighty God, you alone can bring into order the unruly wills and affections of sinners: Grant your people grace to love what you command and desire what you promise; that, among the swift and varied changes of the world, our hearts may surely there be fixed where true joys are to be found; through Jesus Christ our Lord, who lives and reigns with you and the Holy Spirit, one God, now and for ever. Amen.

The Book of Common Prayer

Delight thyself also in the Lord;
and he shall give thee the desires of thine heart.
Commit thy way unto the Lord; trust also in him;
and he shall bring it to pass.

PSALM 37:4-5, KJV

DESIRE ...

Beyond Earth's Best Bliss

"He fulfills the desires of those who fear him" (Psalm 145:19, NIV). As we learn to fear, honor, and reverence Him, our desires themselves are gradually corrected. Things for which we once burned with desire lose their appeal. We learn, in the words of a prayer written in A.D. 492, to love what He commands and to desire nothing that He does not promise. Earth's "best bliss" will never fill our hearts, as Bernard of Clairvaux knew.

Quest for Love

Jesus, Thou joy of loving hearts,
Thou Fount of life, Thou Light of men,
From the best bliss that earth imparts,
We turn unfilled to Thee again.

Bernard of Clairvaux, trans. by Ray Palmer

Thou hast made us for Thyself, O Lord;
and our heart is restless until it rests in Thee.

Augustine of Hippo

Desire

LEADING TO HEAVENLY HAPPINESS

If we truly believe that God wants to bring us to our full glory, we will long increasingly to unite our wills with His. It is in exact proportion as we do this that we will find happiness here on earth. If His will is done on earth, it becomes like heaven, where His will is always done.

A Path Through Suffering

Happiness, Heaven itself, is nothing else but a perfect conformity, a cheerful and eternal compliance of all the powers of the soul with the Will of God.

Samuel Shaw

Desire

LIKE THE BLUEBELLS

As the misty bluebell wood
Very still and shadowy,
Does not seek, far less compel
Several word from several bell,
But lifts up her quiet blue—
So all my desire is before Thee.

For the prayer of human hearts
In the shadow of the Tree,
Various as the various flowers,
Blown by wind and wet by showers,
Rests at last in silent love—
Lord, all my desire is before Thee.

Amy Carmichael, "Bluebells"

DESIRE ...

And the Breath of God

Dear Lord and Father of mankind,
Forgive our feverish ways!
Reclothe us in our rightful mind;
In purer lives Thy service find,
In deeper reverence, praise.

Drop Thy still dews of quietness,
Till all our strivings cease;
Take from our souls the strain and stress,
And let our ordered lives confess
The beauty of Thy peace.

Breathe through the heats of our desire
Thy coolness and Thy balm;
Let sense be dumb, let flesh retire:
Speak through the earthquake, wind, and fire,
O still small voice of calm!

John Greenleaf Whittier

ENDURE ...

With Patience

Teach me to feel that Thou art always nigh;
Teach me the struggles of the soul to bear—
To check the rising doubt, the rebel sigh;
Teach me the patience of unanswered prayer.

George Croly

The Lord will fulfill his purpose for me;
your love, O Lord, endures forever—
do not abandon the works of your hands.

PSALM 138:8

Endure

WITH FAITH

Let nothing disturb you,
Nothing affright you;
All things are passing;
God never changes;
Patient endurance
Attaineth to all things;
Who God possesses
In nothing is wanting;
God alone suffices.

Motto of Teresa of Avila

ENDURE ...

With Courage

One of the nicest things any of the listeners to my broadcast, "Gateway to Joy," has written to me came from a little girl: "You make me brave." Sometimes I wonder what has happened to words like courage and endurance. What reason is there in our feel-comfortable society ever to be brave? Very little, and when you think about it, we miss it, don't we? To be really brave is to lay oneself open to charges of hypocrisy, of being "in denial," or out of touch with one's feelings. Moses charged Joshua to be strong and very courageous. Courage is not the absence of fear but the willingness to do the thing we fear. Go straight into the furnace or the lions' den. Were those men out of touch with their feelings or with reality? No. Nor was the psalmist who said, "When I am afraid, I will trust" (Psalm 56:3, NIV). There's a big difference between feeling and willing.

Keep a Quiet Heart

For some, it is down crosses and up umbrellas, but I am persuaded that we must take heaven with the wind and the rain in our faces.

Letters of Samuel Rutherford

ENDURE ...

With Perspective

When a man conquers his adversaries and his difficulties, it is not as if he never had encountered them. Their power, still kept, is in all his future life. They are not only events in his past history, they are elements in all his present character. His victory is colored with the hard struggle that won it. His sea of glass is always mingled with fire, just as this peaceful crust of the earth on which we live with its wheat fields, and vineyards, and orchards, and flower-beds, is full still of the power of the convulsion that wrought it into its present shape, of the floods and volcanoes and glaciers which have rent it, or drowned it, or tortured it. Just as the whole fruitful earth, deep in its heart, is still mingled with the ever-burning fire that is working out its chemical fitness for its work, just so the life that has been overturned and overturned by the strong hand of God, filled with the deep revolutionary forces of suffering, purified by the strong fires of temptation, keeps its long discipline forever, roots in that discipline the deepest growths of the most sunny and luxuriant spiritual life that it is ever able to attain.

Phillips Brooks

Endure

WITH RENEWED STRENGTH

Long is the way, and very steep the slope,
Strengthen me once again, O God of Hope.

Far, very far, the summit doth appear;
But Thou art near, my God, but Thou art near.

And Thou wilt give me with my daily food,
Powers of endurance, courage, fortitude.

Thy way is perfect; only let that way
Be clear before my feet from day to day.

Thou art my Portion, saith my soul to Thee,
O what a Portion is my God to me.

Amy Carmichael, "Thy Way Is Perfect"

FEAR NOT ...

The Dragons

One particular spot where I lived as a missionary became like a "place of dragons." It was full of things I was afraid of and did not know how to cope with. Once in a while I felt as though I were about to be devoured. "Sore broken" is the psalmist's expression.... I was on my way back to that place one night, camping where we usually did at the junction of two rivers.... Everything was quiet except for the night birds and tree frogs. There was nothing especially distinct about this journey back home. I had made it before. But as I lay in my blanket I began to feel something like what fell on Abraham: "a horror of great darkness." How could I go back to those "dragons"? My heart was about to turn back.

Then I thought of Jesus' words to His disciples: "Lo, I am with you all the days" [Matthew 28:20, Rotherham]. If He was with me then I was certainly with Him. The place of dragons was the place He was taking me, and I was still following—I had not gotten off the track. I was with Him still, sharing in a small measure His cross.

God's Guidance

———————————————————

"Fear not, I am with thee; O be not dismayed,
For I am thy God, and will still give thee aid;
I'll strengthen thee, help thee, and cause thee
 to stand,
Upheld by My righteous, omnipotent hand."

"When through the deep waters I call thee to go,
The rivers of woe shall not thee overflow;
For I will be with thee thy troubles to bless,
And sanctify to thee thy deepest distress."

"When through fiery trials thy pathway shall lie,
My grace, all-sufficient, shall be thy supply,
The flame shall not hurt thee; I only design
Thy dross to consume, and thy gold to refine."

"K" in John Rippon's Selection of Hymns

FEAR NOT ...

Nor Dread the Dark Clouds

God moves in a mysterious way
His wonders to perform;
He plants His footsteps in the sea,
And rides upon the storm.

Ye fearful saints, fresh courage take;
The clouds ye so much dread
Are big with mercy, and shall break
In blessings on your head.

Judge not the Lord by feeble sense,
But trust Him for His grace;
Behind a frowning providence
He hides a smiling face.

Blind unbelief is sure to err,
And scan His work in vain:
God is His own interpreter,
And He will make it plain.

William Cowper

FEAR NOT ...

Through the Age-Long Minute

Thou art the Lord who slept upon the pillow,
Thou art the Lord who soothed the furious sea,
What matter beating wind and tossing billow
If only we are in the boat with Thee?

Hold us in quiet through the age-long minute
While Thou art silent, and the wind is shrill:
Can the boat sink while Thou, dear Lord, art in it?
Can the heart faint that waiteth on Thy will?

Amy Carmichael, "The Age-Long Minute"

Fear Not

GOD'S ASSIGNED TASK

Sometimes a task we have begun takes on seemingly crushing size, and we wonder what ever gave us the notion that we could accomplish it. There is no way out, no way around it, and yet we cannot contemplate actually carrying it through. The rearing of children or the writing of a book are illustrations that come to mind. Let us recall that the task is a divinely appointed one, and divine aid is therefore to be expected. Expect it! Ask for it, wait for it, believe that God gives it. Offer to Him the job itself, along with your fears and misgivings about it. He will not fail or be discouraged. Let His courage encourage you. The day will come when the task will be finished. Trust Him for it.

A Lamp for My Feet

For the Lord God will help me;
therefore shall I not be confounded: therefore have I set my
face like a flint, and I know that I shall not be ashamed.

ISAIAH 50:7, KJV

34

GIVE THANKS ...

For All Good Gifts

We plow the fields, and scatter
The good seed on the land,
But it is fed and watered
By God's almighty hand.

All good gifts around us
Are sent from heaven above;
Then thank the Lord, O thank the Lord,
For all His love.

Matthias Claudius, trans. by Jane Campbell

No gift unrecognized as coming from God is at its own best: therefore many things that God would gladly give us, things even that we need because we are, must wait until we ask for them, that we may know whence they come: when in all gifts we find Him, then in Him we shall find all things.

George MacDonald

With Heart and Hands and Voices

Now thank we all our God
With heart and hands and voices,
Who wondrous things hath done,
In whom His world rejoices;
Who from our mothers' arms
Hath blessed us on our way
With countless gifts of love,
And still is ours today.

O may this bounteous God
Through all our life be near us,
With ever joyful hearts
And blessed peace to cheer us;
And keep us in His grace,
And guide us when perplexed,
And free us from all ills
In this world and the next.

Martin Rinkart, trans. by Catherine Winkworth

Give thanks ...
WITH GRATEFUL MEMORY

We thank Thee, Lord, for the glory of the late days and the excellent face of Thy sun. We thank Thee for good news received. We thank Thee for the pleasures we have enjoyed and for those we have been able to confer. And now, when the clouds gather and rain impends over the forest and our house, permit us not to be cast down; let us not lose the savor of past mercies and past pleasures; but, like the voice of a bird singing in the rain, let grateful memory survive in the hour of darkness.

Robert Louis Stevenson

GIVE THANKS ...

With Grace and Power

Often I pray for someone whose circumstances or needs are unknown to me. There are many prayers in Paul's letters which may be used for almost anyone. One of my favorites is in Colossians 1:9-12. A part of this prayer asks, "May he strengthen you, in his glorious might, with ample power to meet whatever comes with fortitude, patience, and joy, and to give thanks to the Father" (NEB).

That seems to cover every possibility. It does not ask for instant solutions or reversals. It does not call on God for miraculous deliverance out of any trouble that might come. It asks for a truly Christian response, by the sufficient power of God: to meet whatever comes as a true Christian should meet it, with the Holy Spirit's gifts of fortitude, patience, and joy. It asks for the power to give thanks. It takes *power, doesn't it, to thank the Father when everything in us protests? But we find in* Him *(not always in what happens to us) plenty of reason to thank Him and plenty of power.*

A Lamp for My Feet

Give thanks
THAT ONE THING MORE

Thou hast given so much to me,
Give one thing more, a grateful heart....

...I cry, and cry again,
And in no quiet canst Thou be,
Till I a thankful heart obtain
Of Thee.

Not thankful when it pleaseth me,
As if Thy blessings had spare days;
But such a heart whose pulse may be
Thy praise.

George Herbert

HOPE ...

In the God of Hope

Great God of Hope, how green Thy trees,
How calm each several star.
Renew us; make us fresh as these,
Calm as those are.

For what can dim his hope who sees,
Though faintly and afar,
The power that kindles green in trees,
And light in star?

Amy Carmichael, "Hope"

HOPE ...

For Transformation

*N*ote this bit of gorse bush. The whole year round the thorn has been hardening and sharpening. Spring comes; the thorn does not drop off and it does not soften. There it is, as uncompromising as ever, but half-way up appear two brown furry balls, mere specks at first, that break at last—straight out of last year's thorn—into a blaze of fragrant golden glory!

Lilias Trotter

*A*re you sure that your problems baffle the One who since the world began has been bringing flowers from thorns? Your thorns are a different story, are they? You have been brought to a place of self-despair, nothingness. It is hard even to think of any good reason for going on. You live in most unfavorable conditions, with intractable people, you are up against impossible odds. Is this something new? The people of Israel were up against impossible odds when they found themselves between the chariots of Egypt and the Red Sea. Their God is our God. The God of Israel and the God of the gorse thorns looks down on us with love and says, "Nothing has happened to you which is not common to all. I can manage it. Trust Me."

He wants to transform every form of human suffering into something glorious. He can redeem it. He can bring life out of death.... When our souls lie barren in a winter which seems hopeless and endless, God has not abandoned us. His work goes on. He asks our acceptance of the painful process and our trust that He will indeed give resurrection life.

A Path Through Suffering

Hope

SING AND PRAY

If thou but suffer God to guide thee,
And hope in Him through all thy ways,
He'll give thee strength, whate'er betide thee,
And bear thee through the evil days;
Who trusts in God's unchanging love
Builds on the rock that naught can move.

Obey, thou restless heart, be still
And wait in cheerful hope, content
To take whate'er His gracious will,
His all discerning love, hath sent;
Nor doubt our inmost wants are known
To Him who chose us for His own.

Sing, pray, and swerve not from His ways;
But do thine own part faithfully.
Trust His rich promises of grace,
So shall they be fulfilled in thee.
God never yet forsook in need
The soul that trusted Him indeed.

Georg Neumark, trans. by Catherine Winkworth

HOPE ...

With Confidence

Be still my soul: thy best, thy heavenly Friend
Through thorny ways leads to a joyful end.

Be still my soul: thy God doth undertake
To guide the future as He has the past.
Thy hope, thy confidence let nothing shake;
All now mysterious shall be bright at last.

Katherine von Schlegel, trans. by Jane Borthwick

Set your hope fully on the grace to be given you
when Jesus Christ is revealed.

1 PETER 1:13

43

INTERCEDE ...

With the Worldwide Church

When newly married and living in a little palm-thatched house in the jungle, Jim Elliot and I remembered that even in so remote a place we were still gathered in that great communion [of saints], and we used often to sing "The Day Thou Gavest, Lord, Is Ended."

Keep a Quiet Heart

We thank Thee that Thy church, unsleeping
While earth rolls onward into light,
Through all the world her watch is keeping,
And rests not now by day or night.

As o'er each continent and island
The dawn leads on another day,
The voice of prayer is never silent,
Nor dies the strain of praise away.

John Ellerton

INTERCEDE ...

For Our Children

Father, hear us, we are praying,
Hear the words our hearts are saying,
We are praying for our children.

Keep them from the powers of evil,
From the secret, hidden peril,
From the whirlpool that would suck them,
From the treacherous quicksand, pluck them.

From the worldling's hollow gladness,
From the sting of faithless sadness,
Holy Father, save our children.

Through life's troubled waters steer them,
Through life's bitter battle cheer them,
Father, Father, be Thou near them.
Read the language of our longing,
Read the wordless pleadings thronging,
Holy Father, for our children.

Amy Carmichael, from "For Our Children"

INTERCEDE ...

For Our Children's Future Mates

*K*atherine Morgan told me that when her daughters were born, she began to pray for the mothers of the men they would marry. I had never thought of such a prayer, but I recommend it to you mothers of young children. Probably your children's spouses are growing up now, too. Will their mothers (and fathers) do a good and faithful job as parents? What a difference it will make in the homes your children establish if they do!

Newsletter

*The prayer of a righteous man
is powerful and effective.*

JAMES 5:16

Intercede ...
FOR OUR HUSBANDS

Lord, grant me the vision of a true lover as I look at ____. Help me to see him through Your eyes, to read the thoughts he does not put into words, to bear with his human imperfections, remembering that he bears with mine and that You are at work in both of us. Thank You, Lord, for this man, Your carefully chosen gift to me, and for the high privilege of being heirs together of the grace of life. Help me to make it as easy and pleasant as I possibly can for him to do Your will.

Newsletter

Intercede

A Parting Prayer

Care Thou for mine whom I must leave behind;
Care that they know who 'tis for them takes care;
Thy present patience help them still to bear;
Lord, keep them clearing, growing, heart and mind;
In one Thy oneness us together bind;
Last earthly prayer with which to Thee I cling—
Grant that, save love, we owe not anything.

George MacDonald

JOY ...

In Suffering

God ...
Setteth in pain the jewel of His joy.

F.W.H. Meyers

A friend who is gravely ill ... is greatly loved by many and has had a unique ministry because of her gifts of friendship and hospitality. Must she suffer?

The answer is yes. For the Lord who loves her suffered and wants her to fellowship with Himself. The joy of thus knowing Him comes not in spite of but because of suffering, just as resurrection comes out of death. I have a Savior because I am a sinner; a beauty is given the child of God in exchange for ashes.

We want to avoid suffering, death, sin, ashes. But we live in a world crushed and broken and torn, a world God Himself visited to redeem. We receive His poured-out life, and being allowed the high privilege of suffering with Him, may then pour ourselves out for others.

How can one's illness help another? By being offered to Him who can transform it into blessing.

A Lamp for My Feet

O Joy that seekest me through pain,
I cannot close my heart to Thee;
I trace the rainbow through the rain,
And feel the promise is not vain
That morn shall tearless be.

George Matheson

In Song

Sometimes a light surprises
The Christian while he sings;
It is the Lord who rises
With Healing in his wings:
When comforts are declining,
He grants the soul again
A season of clear shining
To cheer it after rain.

Though vine, nor fig tree neither,
Their wonted fruit should bear,
Though all the fields should wither,
Nor flocks, nor herds, be there:
Yet God the same abiding,
His praise shall tune my voice;
For while in him confiding,
I cannot but rejoice.

William Cowper

JOY ...

In the Rhythms of Life

The Bible is full of commands to be joyful. The Lord commanded the people of Israel to set aside certain days for celebration, and on those days they were to rejoice. There was no provision made for any who might not happen to "feel like" rejoicing. This was what they were to do, young and old, slaves and free, aliens, orphans, and widows—in obedience to the command....

The rhythm of life is one of God's mercies, meant to keep us from sinking into individual ruts. We are called away from our personal inclination by the dawning of each new day, by the sun's going down so that we may cease from our work, by the changing seasons which require changes of habit, work, and dress, and by the regular occurrence of "feasts" when, without reference to how we happen to feel, we may join with others in purposeful rejoicing. We may choose to be glad.

A Lamp for My Feet

JOY ...

Everlasting

Make a joyful noise unto the Lord, all ye lands.
Serve the Lord with gladness:
come before his presence with singing.
Know ye that the Lord, he is God:
it is he that hath made us,
and not we ourselves;
we are his people,
and the sheep of his pasture.
Enter into his gates with thanksgiving,
and into his courts with praise:
be thankful unto him,
and bless his name.
For the Lord is good;
his mercy is everlasting;
and his truth endureth to all generations.

PSALM 100, KJV

KNEEL ...

With Open Heart

Create in me a pure heart, O God,
and renew a steadfast spirit within me.
Do not cast me from your presence
or take your Holy Spirit from me.
Restore to me the joy of your salvation
and grant me a willing spirit, to sustain me.

PSALM 51:10-12

Almighty God, to you all hearts are open, all desires known, and from you no secrets are hid: Cleanse the thoughts of our hearts by the inspiration of your Holy Spirit, that we may perfectly love you, and worthily magnify your holy Name; through Christ our Lord. Amen.

The Book of Common Prayer

KNEEL ...

With Open Hands

There are moments when, whatever be the attitude of the body, the soul is on its knees.

Victor Hugo

When vision fadeth, and the sense of things,
And powers dissolve like colours in the air,
And no more can I bring Thee offerings,
Nor any ordered prayer,

Then, like a wind blowing from Paradise,
Falleth a healing word upon mine ear,
Let the lifting up of my hands be as the evening sacrifice;
The Lord doth hear.

Amy Carmichael, "The Lifting Up of Hands"

Kneel

BEGGING MERCY

Christians in the Orthodox Church use a prayer called the Jesus Prayer. Sometimes *they pray it in the rhythm of breathing, learning in this way almost to "pray without ceasing." The words are simple, but they cover everything we need to ask for ourselves and others:* Lord Jesus Christ, Son of God, have mercy on us.

The Lord did not say we should not use repetition. He said we should not use vain repetition. A prayer prayed from the heart of the child to the Father is never vain....

The Jesus Prayer was one my husband Add and I often used together when he was dying of cancer, when we seemed to have "used up" all the other prayers. I recommend it to you.

Keep a Quiet Heart

KNEEL ...

Requesting Strength

From moral weakness of spirit; from timidity; from hesitation; from fear of men and dread of responsibility, strengthen us with courage to speak the truth in love and self-control; and alike from the weakness of hasty violence and weakness of moral cowardice,
Save us and help us, we humbly beseech Thee, O Lord.

From weakness of judgment; from the indecision that can make no choice; from the irresolution that carries no choice into act; and from losing opportunities to serve Thee,
Save us and help us, we humbly beseech Thee, O Lord.

From the Southwell Litany for the Personal Life

KNEEL ...

Asking for Grace to Age Well

Lord, You know better than I know myself that I am getting older and will someday be old. Keep me from … the fatal habit of thinking I must say something on every subject and on every occasion. Release me from craving to straighten out everybody's affairs. Make me thoughtful but not moody, helpful but not bossy. With my vast store of wisdom it seems a pity not to use it all, but You know, Lord, that I want a few friends at the end. Keep my mind from the recital of endless details—give me wings to come to the point. Seal my lips on my aches and pains. They are increasing, and my love of rehearsing them is becoming sweeter. I dare not ask for grace enough to enjoy the tales of others' pains, but help me to endure them with patience. I dare not ask for improved memory, but for a growing humility and a lessening cocksureness when my memory seems to clash with the memories of others. Teach me the glorious lesson that occasionally I may be mistaken. Keep me reasonably sweet. I do not want to be a saint—some of them are so hard to live with—but a sour old woman is one of the crowning works of the devil. Give me the ability to see good things in unexpected places, and talents in unexpected people. And give me the grace to tell them so.

Anonymous, often attributed to a seventeenth-century nun

LOVE ...

The Lover of My Soul

Loved with everlasting love,
Led by grace that love to know;
Spirit, breathing from above,
Thou hast taught me it is so!
Oh, this full and perfect peace!
Oh, this transport all divine!
In a love which cannot cease,
I am His, and He is mine.

Things that once were wild alarms
Cannot now disturb my rest;
Closed in everlasting arms,
Pillowed on the loving breast.
Oh, to lie forever here,
Doubt, and care, and self resign,
While He whispers in my ear,
I am His, and He is mine.

George Wade Robinson

LOVE ...

Through Me

There is a quiet, steadying power—the love of Christ, and "this love of which I speak is slow to lose patience—it looks for a way of being constructive" (1 Corinthians 13:4, Phillips). It is not in me. That brand of love is not a part of my nature. So I simply ask for it. Lord, Your love alone, at work in me, behaves like that.

A Lamp for My Feet

Love through me, Love of God,
Make me like Thy clear air
Through which unhindered, colours pass
As though it were not there.

Amy Carmichael, from "Love Through Me"

LOVE ...

Daily

True love is but a humble, low-born thing,
And hath its food served up in earthenware;
It is a thing to walk with, hand in hand,
Through the everydayness of this work-day world,
Baring its tender feet to every roughness,
Yet letting not one heart-beat go astray
From beauty's law of plainness and content—
A simple, fireside thing, whose quiet smile
Can warm earth's poorest hovel to a home.

James Russell Lowell

Now that you have purified yourselves by obeying the truth so that you have sincere love for your brothers, love one another deeply, from the heart.

1 Peter 1:22

LOVE ...

Simply, Broadly

For the love of God is broader
Than the measure of man's mind;
And the heart of the Eternal
Is most wonderfully kind.

But we make His love too narrow
By false limits of our own
And we magnify its strictness,
With a zeal He will not own.

If our love were but more simple,
We should take Him at His word....

Frederick W. Faber

Love

WITH COURAGE

God's love holds us to the highest. This was the kind of love Amy Carmichael of India prayed for and taught to the children on Dohnavur—this love, the kind wherewith God loved us. "Hold one another to the highest," she told them. God's purpose was to lift us out of ourselves, out of the miry clay, and set our feet on a rock. We are not saviors, but we can help others toward faith. This means not only loving them while they're still in the mire, but loving them out of it. We must love them as they are and love them enough to draw them higher.

Someone has said that the best thing a father can do for his children is to love their mother. This demonstration far outshines all the homilies he can preach at them. By daily example he holds them to the highest. Jesus said, "For their sakes I sanctify myself" (John 17:19, KJV). His holy obedience to the Father saved us. Our holy obedience to the Father makes a difference to those we love.

Lord, give me the courage to love as You loved me.

A Lamp for My Feet

MEDITATE ...

Set Aside Time for God

*I*t is a good and necessary thing to set aside time for God in each day. The busier the day, the more indispensable is the quiet period for prayer, Bible reading, and silent listening. It often happens, however, that I find my mind so full of earthly matters that it seems I have gotten up early in vain and have wasted three-fourths of the time so dearly bought (I do love my sleep!). But I have come to believe that the act of will required to arrange time for God may be an offering to Him. As such He accepts it, and what would otherwise be "loss" to me I count as "gain" for Christ. Let us not be "weary in well-doing," or discouraged in the pursuit of holiness. Let us, like Moses, go to the Rock of Horeb—and God says to us what He said to him, "You will find me waiting for you there" (Exodus 17:6, NEB).

A Lamp for My Feet

I will meditate in thy precepts.

PSALM 119:78, KJV

63

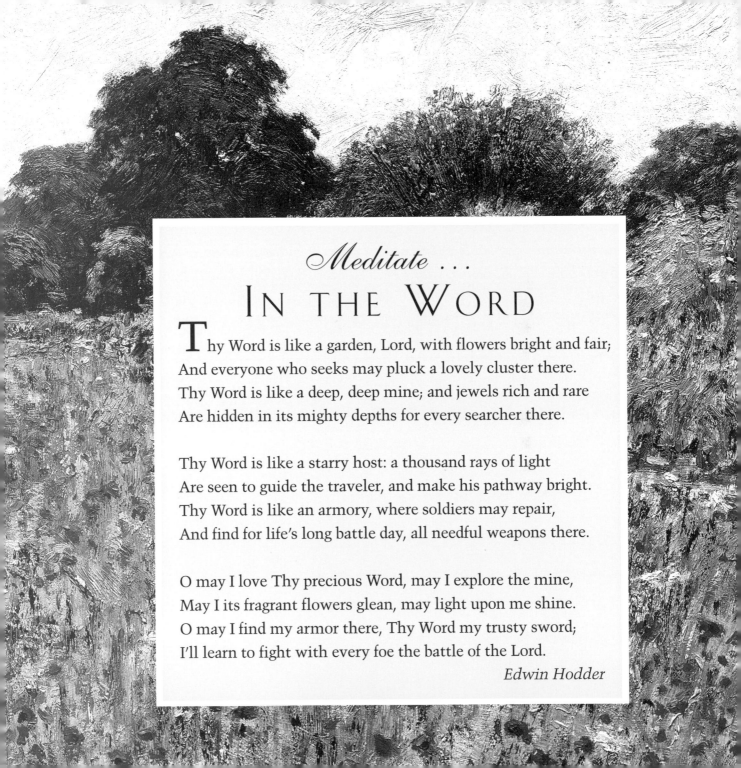

Meditate ...
IN THE WORD

Thy Word is like a garden, Lord, with flowers bright and fair;
And everyone who seeks may pluck a lovely cluster there.
Thy Word is like a deep, deep mine; and jewels rich and rare
Are hidden in its mighty depths for every searcher there.

Thy Word is like a starry host: a thousand rays of light
Are seen to guide the traveler, and make his pathway bright.
Thy Word is like an armory, where soldiers may repair,
And find for life's long battle day, all needful weapons there.

O may I love Thy precious Word, may I explore the mine,
May I its fragrant flowers glean, may light upon me shine.
O may I find my armor there, Thy Word my trusty sword;
I'll learn to fight with every foe the battle of the Lord.

Edwin Hodder

MEDITATE ...

Hear and Mark the Word

Blessed Lord, who caused all holy Scriptures to be written for our learning: Grant us so to hear them, read, mark, learn, and inwardly digest them, that we may embrace and ever hold fast the blessed hope of everlasting life, which you have given us in our Savior Jesus Christ; who lives and reigns with you and the Holy Spirit, one God, for ever and ever. Amen.

The Book of Common Prayer

O God, whose Son Jesus is the good shepherd of your people: Grant that when we hear his voice we may know him who calls us each by name, and follow where he leads; who, with you and the Holy Spirit, lives and reigns, one God, for ever and ever. Amen.

The Book of Common Prayer

MEDITATE ...

Learn and Recognize the Word

I have never heard any voices or seen any visions from heaven, but I have been reminded "out of the blue" on more occasions than I can count of some word from the Bible that exactly suited my need....

When a shortwave radio message told me many years ago that my husband and four friends were missing in the jungle, the words of Isaiah 43:1-3 came to me almost as if they had been spoken aloud, but they were words I had memorized years before:

> *Fear not: for I have redeemed thee, I have called thee by thy name; thou art mine. When thou passest through the waters, I will be with thee; and through the rivers, they shall not overflow thee: when thou walkest through the fire, thou shalt not be burned; neither shall the flame kindle upon thee. For I am the Lord thy God.*

These old words came with a power and an insistence that convinced me they came from God, and with them came the faith to believe they were true. However the word comes to our attention, if it is God's truth for us at the time, we are given that assurance.

God's Guidance

MEDITATE ...

On the Mystery of the Incarnation

That the Great Angel-blinding Light should shrink
His blaze, to shine in a poor Shepherd's eye;
That the unmeasur'd God so low should sink,
As Pris'ner in a few poor rags to lie;
That from His Mother's Breast He milk should drink,
Who feeds with Nectar Heaven's fair family,
That a vile Manger His low Bed should prove
Who in a Throne of stars thunders above;
That He whom the Sun serves, should faintly peep
Through clouds of Infant Flesh! That He, the old
Eternal Word, should be a Child, and weep;
That He who made the fire, should fear the cold,
That Heaven's high Majesty His Court should keep
In a clay cottage, by each blast control'd;
That Glories self should serve our Griefs and fears,
And free Eternity submit to years,
Let our overwhelming wonder be.

Richard Crashaw

Nurture

AND MODEL BY EXAMPLE

A careful woman I ought to be;
a little girl follows me.
I do not dare to go astray,
for fear she'll go the selfsame way.
Not once can I escape her eyes;
whate'er she sees me do, she tries.
Like me, she says she's going to be
that little girl who follows me.
I must remember as I go
through summer sun and winter snow,
I'm molding for the years to be
that little girl who follows me.

Author Unknown

NURTURE ...

Faithfully, Graciously

Said one whose yoke
Was that of common folk,
Would that I were like Saint Cecilia,
And could invent some goodly instrument
Passing all yet contrived to worship Thee,
And send a love-song singing over land and sea.

But when I seem
Almost to touch my dream,
I hear a call, persistent though so small,
The which if I ignore, clamours about my door
And bids me run to meet some human need.
Meanwhile my dream drifts off like down of thistle seed.

A sound of gentle stillness stirred and said,
My child, be comforted,
Dear is the offering of melody,
But dearer far, love's lowliest ministry.

Amy Carmichael, "In Any House"

NURTURE ...

And Consider ...

In a book called *Father and Son,* my grandfather, Philip E. Howard, writes:

> Do you remember that encouraging word of Thomas Fuller's, a chaplain of Oliver Cromwell's time? It's a good passage for a father in all humility and gratitude to tuck away in his memory treasures:

Lord, I find the genealogy of my Savior strangely checkered with four remarkable changes in four immediate generations. (1) Rehoboam begat Abijah; that is, a bad father begat a bad son. (2) Abijah begat Asa; that is, a bad father begat a good son. (3) Asa begat Jehoshaphat; that is, a good father a good son. (4) Jehoshaphat begat Joram; that is, a good father a bad son. I see, Lord, from hence that my father's piety cannot be entailed; that is bad news for me. But I see also that actual impiety is not always hereditary; that is good news for my son.

NURTURE ...

And Eventually Let Go

*R*elinquishment is always a part of the process of maturing. When Christian parents have done all that can be done to shape their children for God, the time comes when the hands must let go. The child, now a responsible adult, must be released. For any parent this is painful, even when the child is moving in the direction the parents prayed for. The child's continued development, and the spiritual health of the parents as well, depend on the willingness to accept this next stage of the cycle—hands off, ready to part without a struggle, giving up authority and control, entrusting that child to God.

A Path Through Suffering

NURTURE ...

And Pray

After my mother's death I found a little red notebook in which she had copied this "grandparent's prayer."

Holy Father, in Thy mercy, hear our anxious prayer;
Keep our loved ones, now far distant, 'neath Thy care.

Jesus, Savior, let Thy presence be their light and guide;
Keep, O keep them, in their weakness, at Thy side.

When in sorrow, when in danger, when in loneliness,
In Thy love look down and comfort their distress.

May the joy of Thy salvation be their strength and stay;
May they love and may they praise Thee day by day.

Holy Spirit, let Thy teaching sanctify their life;
Send Thy grace that they may conquer in the strife.

Father, Son, and Holy Spirit, God the One in Three,
Bless them, guide them, save them, keep them near to Thee.

I.S. Stevenson

AND LIGHTEN THE LOAD

*L*et us remember that it is not God who makes many of the crosses that we find in our way, such as we commonly call "crosses." Our Heavenly Father makes "straight paths for our feet." ... But when the path that God points out goes north and south, and our stubborn wills lead us east and west, the consequence is *"a cross"*—a cross of our own making, not that which our Master bids us "take up and carry after Him," and of which it has been well said, "He always carries the heaviest end Himself."

Annie Webb-Peploe

OBEY ...

In the Face of Temptation

Y ou have to ask for help. Help will most certainly be given. When I pray for this, sometimes the words of an old gospel song that we used to sing in family prayers come to my aid:

> Yield not to temptation, for yielding is sin.
> Each victory will help you some other to win.
> Fight manfully onward, dark passions subdue.
> Look ever to Jesus, He will carry you through.
>
> Ask the Savior to help you,
> Comfort, strengthen, and keep you;
> He is willing to aid you,
> He will carry you through.

Horatio Palmer

T he song is called *"Yield Not to Temptation."* It is the yielding, not the temptation itself, that is sin. We have to keep asking the Savior to help us, comfort, strengthen, and keep us. He is not reluctant. He is willing. He will carry you through, if you want to be carried through. You must want to.

Passion and Purity

OBEY ...

And Trust ... for Joy

But we never can prove
The delights of His love
Until all on the altar we lay;
For the favor He shows,
And the joy He bestows,
Are for them who will trust and obey.

Trust and obey, for there's no other way
To be happy in Jesus, but to trust and obey.

John Sammis

Obey . . .
WITH DELIGHT

O Lord, renew our spirits and draw our hearts unto Yourself, that our work may not be to us a burden but a delight; and give us such a mighty love to You as may sweeten our obedience. O let us not serve You with the spirit of bondage as slaves, but with cheerfulness and gladness, delighting in You and rejoicing in Your work.

Benjamin Jenks

OBEY ...

Without Interruption

Lord, do Thou turn me all into love,
and all my love into obedience
and let my obedience be
without interruption.

Jeremy Taylor

*If anyone loves me, he will obey my teaching.
My Father will love him, and we will come to him
and make our home with him.*

JOHN 14:23

Draw Nearer to God

For flowers unsought, in desert places
Flashing enchantment on the sight;
For radiance on familiar faces
As they passed upward into light;

For blessings of the fruitful season,
For work and rest, for friends and home,
For the great gifts of thought and reason—
To praise and bless Thee, Lord, we come.

And when we gather up the story
Of all Thy mercies flowing free,
Crown of them all, that hope of glory,
Of growing ever nearer Thee.

Eliza Scudder

PRAISE ...

At Dawn: Through All the Ages Long

When morning gilds the skies,
My heart awakening cries:
    May Jesus Christ be praised;
Alike at work or prayer
To Jesus I repair:
    May Jesus Christ be praised.

Does sadness fill my mind?
A solace here I find:
    May Jesus Christ be praised;
Or fades my earthly bliss?
My comfort still is this:
    May Jesus Christ be praised.

Be this, while life is mine,
My canticle divine,
    May Jesus Christ be praised;
Be this th'eternal song,
Through all the ages long:
    May Jesus Christ be praised.

From German, trans. by Edward Caswall

Praise

AND DELIGHT GOD

*T*he third stanza of "O Worship the King" delights me. It must delight God when I sing it to Him:

> Thy bountiful care, what tongue can recite?
> It breathes in the air, it shines in the light;
> It streams from the hills, it descends to the plain,
> And sweetly distills in the dew and the rain.

That's praise. By putting into words things on earth for which we thank Him, we are training ourselves to be ever more aware of such things as we live our lives. It is easy otherwise to be oblivious of the thousand evidences of His care. Have you thought of thanking God for light and air, because in them His care breathes and shines?

On Asking God Why

Praise ...

ALL MY DAYS

I praise Thee while my days go on;
I love Thee while my days go on:
Through dark and dearth, through fire and frost,
With emptied arms and treasure lost,
I thank Thee while my days go on.

Elizabeth Barrett Browning

PRAISE ...

And Conquer

We see not yet all things put under Thee,
We see not yet the glory that shall be,
We see not yet, and yet by faith we see,
Alleluia, Alleluia.

We see the shadows gathering for flight,
The powers of dawn dispel the brooding night,
The steadfast march of the triumphant light,
Alleluia.

Be we in East or West, or North, or South,
By wells of water, or in land of drouth,
Lo, Thou hast put a new song in our mouth,
Alleluia.

Therefore we triumph, therefore we are strong,
Though vision tarry, and the night be long,
For lifted up, we conquer by Thy song,
Alleluia.

Amy Carmichael, "We Conquer by His Song"

QUIET ...

My Heart

Lord, give to me a quiet heart
That does not ask to understand,
But confident steps forward in
The darkness guided by Thy hand.

Keep a Quiet Heart

Quiet, Lord, my froward heart.
Make me teachable and mild,
    upright, simple, free from art.
Make me as a weaned child.
From distrust and enemy free,
    pleased with all that pleaseth Thee.

John Newton

QUIET ...

My Mind

What room is there for troubled fear?
I know my Lord, and He is near;
And He will light my candle, so
That I may see the way to go.

There need be no bewilderment
To one who goes where he is sent;
The trackless plain by night and day
Is set with signs, lest he should stray....

My path may lead through woods at night,
Where neither moon nor any light
Of guiding star or beacon shines;
He will not let me miss my signs.

Lord, grant to me a quiet mind,
That trusting Thee, for Thou art kind,
I may go on without a fear,
For Thou, my Lord, art always near.

Amy Carmichael, from "A Quiet Mind"

Quiet

MY OUTLOOK

Calmly we look behind us,
    on joys and sorrows past,
We know that all is mercy now,
    and shall be well at last;
Calmly we look before us—
    we fear no future ill,
Enough for safety and for peace,
    if Thou art with us still.

Jane Borthwick

QUIET ...

The Vexatious Spirit

What if the wicked nature, which is as a sea casting out mire and dirt, rage against thee? There is a river, a sweet, still, flowing river, the streams whereof will make glad thy heart. And learn but in quietness and stillness to retire to the Lord, and wait upon Him, in whom thou shalt feel peace and joy, in the midst of thy trouble from the cruel and vexatious spirit of this world.

Isaac Penington

Often a Christian man or woman falls prey to that cruel and vexatious spirit, wondering how ... who, when, where? It is on God that we should wait, as a waiter waits—not for but on the customer—alert, watchful, attentive, with no agenda of his own, ready to do whatever is wanted. "My soul, wait thou only upon God; for my expectation is from him" (Psalm 62:5, KJV). In Him alone lie our security, our confidence, our trust. A spirit of restlessness and resistance can never wait, but one who believes he is loved with an everlasting love, and knows that underneath are the everlasting arms, will find strength and peace.

Quest for Love

QUIET ...

Before God

I wait.
Dear Lord, Thy ways
Are past finding out,
Thy love too high.
O hold me still
Beneath Thy shadow.
It is enough that Thou
Lift up the light
Of Thy countenance.
I wait—
Because I am commanded
So to do. My mind
Is filled with wonderings.
My soul asks "Why?"
But then the quiet word,
"Wait thou only
Upon God."
And so, not even for the light
To show a step ahead,
But for Thee, dear Lord,
I wait.

Passion and Purity

REPENT ...

And Accept God's Grace

Marvelous grace of our loving Lord,
Grace that exceeds our sin and our guilt,
Yonder on Calvary's mount outpoured,
There where the blood of the Lamb was spilt.

Sin and despair like the sea waves cold,
Threaten the soul with infinite loss;
Grace that is greater, yes, grace untold,
Points to the Refuge, the mighty Cross.

Dark is the stain that we cannot hide,
What can avail to wash it away?
Look! There is flowing a crimson tide;
Whiter than snow you may be today.

Julia H. Johnston

REPENT...

And Confess

Almighty and most merciful Father,
we have erred and strayed from thy ways like lost sheep,
we have followed too much the devices and desires of our own hearts,
we have offended against thy holy laws,
we have left undone those things which we ought to have done,
and we have done those things which we ought not to have done.
But thou, O Lord, have mercy upon us,
spare thou those who confess their faults,
restore thou those who are penitent,
according to thy promises declared unto mankind
in Christ Jesus our Lord;
and grant, O most merciful Father, for his sake,
that we may hereafter live a godly, righteous, and sober life,
to the glory of thy holy Name. Amen.

The Book of Common Prayer

Repent

AND RECEIVE

My friend Calvin Thielman ... tells the story of an old Scottish preacher who, as he was serving the bread and wine of the Lord's Supper, noticed a young girl sobbing at the communion rail. As he passed her the bread, visible sign of the body of the Lord Jesus ("I give it for the life of the world," He said), the girl turned away her face, which was wet with tears.

"Tak' it, lassie," said the old man. "It's for sinners."

Passion and Purity

REPENT ...

And Make Moment-by-Moment Choices

At the age of ten, I wanted to be born again. It was very simple. I took God at His word, "received" Him, and was given the power to become a child of His. I sang songs like

At the Cross, at the Cross,
Where I first saw the light,
And the burden of my heart rolled away,
It was there by faith I received my sight,
And now I am happy all the day.

(Ralph Hudson)

I cannot claim that overnight I became "happy all the day," but the Spirit of God began to show me that my once-in-a-lifetime choice must be followed by moment-by-moment choices to do things His way or mine. I must accept not just "salvation," meaning a free ticket to heaven, but His sovereign lordship of my life, His will.

A Path Through Suffering

REPENT ...

And Renew

O direct my life towards Thy commandments, hallow my soul, purify my body, correct my thoughts, cleanse my desires, soul and body, mind and spirit, heart and reins. Renew me thoroughly, O Lord, for if Thou wilt Thou canst.

Lancelot Andrewes

It is when the death of winter has done its work that the sun can draw out in each plant its own individuality, and make its existence full and fragrant. Spiritual growth means something more than the sweeping away of the old leaves of sin—it means the life of the Lord Jesus developed in us.

Lilias Trotter

SURRENDER ...

In Meekness

Meekness is teachability. "The meek will he teach his way" (Psalm 25:9, KJV). It is the readiness to be shown, which includes the readiness to lay down my fixed notions, my objections and "what ifs" or "but what abouts," my certainties about the rightness of what I have always done or thought or said. It is the child's glad "Show me! Is this the way? Please help me." We won't make it into the kingdom without that childlikeness, that simple willingness to be taught and corrected and helped. "Receive with meekness the engrafted word, which is able to save your souls" (James 1:21, KJV). Meekness is an explicitly spiritual quality, a fruit of the Spirit, learned, not inherited. It shows in the kind of attention we pay to one another, the tone of voice we use, the facial expression.

Keep a Quiet Heart

Right gladly would He free them from their misery, but He knows only one way: He will teach them to be like Himself, meek and lowly, bearing with gladness the yoke of His Father's will. This is the one, the only right, the only possible way of freeing them from their sin, the cause of their unrest.

George MacDonald

Surrender

TO CHRIST

O *ne morning I was reading the story of Jesus' feeding of the five thousand. The disciples could find only five loaves of bread and two fishes. "Let me have them," said Jesus. He asked for all. He took them, said the blessing, and broke them before He gave them out. I remembered what a chapel speaker, Ruth Stull of Peru, had said: "If my life is broken when given to Jesus, it is because pieces will feed a multitude, while a loaf will satisfy only a little lad."*

Passion and Purity

L ord, teach us to be generous: Teach us to serve You as You deserve; to give and not to count the cost; to fight and not to heed the wounds; to toil and not to seek for rest; to labor and not to ask for reward, save that of knowing that we are doing Your will.

Ignatius of Loyola

Surrender ...

MAKE ME AN INSTRUMENT

Lord, make me an instrument
of Your peace.
Where there is hatred, let me sow love,
Where there is injury, pardon;
Where there is doubt, faith;
Where there is darkness, light;
Where there is sadness, joy.
O divine Master, grant that I may not
so much seek
To be consoled, as to console,
To be understood, as to understand,
To be loved, as to love,
For it is in giving that we receive;
It is in pardoning that we are pardoned;
It is in dying that we are born to eternal life.

Francis of Assisi

SURRENDER ...

And Die to Self

Receive every inward and outward trouble, every disappointment, pain, uneasiness, temptation, darkness, and desolation with both thy hands, as a true opportunity and blessed occasion of dying to self, and entering into a fuller fellowship with thy self-denying, suffering Savior. Look at no inward or outward trouble in any other view; reject every other thought about it; and then every kind of trial and distress will become the blessed day of thy prosperity. That state is best, which exerciseth the highest faith in and fullest resignation to God.

William Law

The only escape from self-love is self-surrender. *"Whoever loses his life for me will find it"* (Matthew 16:25, NIV).

Keep a Quiet Heart

SURRENDER ...

With Willing Spirit

Give me the love that leads the way,
The faith that nothing can dismay,
The hope no disappointments tire,
The passion that will burn like fire,
Let me not sink to be a clod:
Make me Thy fuel, Flame of God.

Amy Carmichael, from "Make Me Thy Fuel"

God, I pray Thee, light these idle sticks of my life and may I burn for Thee. Consume my life, my God, for it is Thine. I seek not a long life, but a full one, like You, Lord Jesus.

Jim Elliot, from Shadow of the Almighty

TRUST ...

The God Who Guides the Birds

To a Water Fowl:

There is a Power whose care
Teaches thy way along the pathless coast—
The desert and illimitable air—
Lone wandering, but not lost....

Thou art gone, the abyss of heaven
Hath swallowed up thy form; yet, on my heart
Deeply hath sunk the lesson thou hast given,
And shall not soon depart.

He who, from zone to zone,
Guides through the boundless sky thy certain flight,
In the long way that I must tread alone,
Will lead my steps aright.

William Cullen Bryant

TRUST ...

Stand Still and See

I'm standing, Lord:
There is a mist that blinds my sight.
Steep, jagged rocks, front, left and right,
Lower, dim, gigantic, in the night.
     Where is the way?...

I'm standing, Lord:
The rock is hard beneath my feet;
I nearly slipped, Lord, on the sleet.
So weary, Lord! and where a seat?
     Still must I stand?

He answered me, and on His face
A look ineffable of grace,
Of perfect, understanding love,
Which all my murmuring did remove.

     I'm standing, Lord:
Since Thou hast spoken, Lord, I see
Thou hast beset—these rocks are Thee!
And since Thy love encloses me,
     I stand and sing.

Betty Scott Stam, "Stand Still and See"

Fear ye not, stand still, and see the salvation of the Lord.

Exodus 14:13, KJV

99

TRUST...

And Bind Yourself to God

I bind unto myself the name,
The strong name of the Trinity;
By invocation of the same,
The Three in One, the One in Three....

I bind unto myself today
The power of God to hold and lead,
His eye to watch, His might to stay,
His ear to hearken to my need.

Christ be with me, Christ within me,
Christ behind me, Christ before me,
Christ beside me, Christ to win me,
Christ to comfort and restore me,
Christ beneath me, Christ above me,
Christ in quiet, Christ in danger,
Christ in mouth of friend or stranger.

Patrick of Ireland,
trans. by Cecil Frances Alexander

TRUST ...

God's Goodness

O Lord, whose way is perfect, help us, we pray, always to trust in Your goodness, that walking with You and following You in all simplicity, we may possess quiet and contented minds and may cast all our care on You, who cares for us. Grant this, O Lord, for Your dear Son's sake, Jesus Christ.

Christina Rossetti

The deep peace that comes from deep trust in God's lovingkindness is not destroyed even by the worst of circumstances, for those Everlasting Arms are still cradling us, we are always "under the Mercy." Corrie ten Boom was "born to trouble" like the rest of us, but in a German concentration camp she jumped to her feet every morning and exuberantly sang "Stand Up, Stand Up for Jesus!" She thanked the Lord for the little parade of ants that marched through her cell, bringing her company. When Paul and Silas were in prison, they prayed and sang. It isn't troubles that make saints, but their response to troubles.

Keep a Quiet Heart

THIS CARE, THIS MOMENT

The care that is filling your mind at this moment, or but waiting till you lay the book aside to leap upon you—that need which is no need—is a demon sucking at the spring of your life.

"No, mine is a reasonable care—an unavoidable care, indeed!"

"Is it something you have to do this very moment?"

"No."

"Then you are allowing it to usurp the place of something that is required of you this moment!"

"There is nothing required of me at this moment."

"Nay, but there is—the greatest thing that can be required of man."

"Pray, what is it?"

"Trust in the living God...."

"I do trust Him in spiritual matters."

"Everything is an affair of the spirit...."

George MacDonald

UNDERSTAND ...

God's Love

hat was I, a jungle missionary, to say to my own child of two when she learned the song "Jesus Loves Me" and wanted to know whether Jesus had loved her daddy too? I gave her the truth: yes. Next question: Then why did He let the Auca Indians kill him? A little girl can be shown that her father's death is a gateway to life for him, but how was I to explain the truth of the delivering power of death? I could not. But I still had to give an answer, a truthful answer: I did not know all God's reasons. The ones I was quite sure I did know Valerie could not have understood then. But that He had reasons, I was sure. That they were loving reasons I was also sure. The assurance that it was not for nothing comforted me and I gave my peace to my child.

A Path Through Suffering

UNDERSTAND ...

God's Generosity

And shall I fear
That there is anything that men hold dear
Thou would'st deprive me of,
And nothing give in place?

That is not so—
For I can see Thy face
And hear Thee now:

"My child, I died for thee.
And if the gift of love and life
You took from Me,
Shall I one precious thing withhold—
One beautiful and bright,
One pure and precious thing withhold?
My child, it cannot be."

Betty Scott Stam, "My Testimony," 1929

UNDERSTAND ...

God's Sovereignty

All of the past, I believe, is a part of God's story of each child of His—a mystery of love and sovereignty, written before the foundation of the world, never a hindrance to the task He has designed for us, but rather the very preparation suited to our particular personality's need.

...*"It is the glory of God to conceal a matter"* (Proverbs 25:2, NIV). God conceals much that we do not need to know, yet we do know that He calls His own sheep by name and leads them out. When does that begin? Does the Shepherd overlook anything that the sheep need?

Keep a Quiet Heart

Nothing else but this seeing God in everything will make us loving and patient with those who annoy and trouble us. They will be to us then only the instruments for accomplishing His tender and wise purposes towards us, and we shall even find ourselves at last inwardly thanking them for the blessings they bring us.

Nothing else will completely put an end to all murmuring or rebelling thoughts.

Hannah Whitall Smith

Understand ... GOD'S ANSWERS

I have often asked why. Many things have happened which I didn't plan on and which human rationality could not explain. In the darkness of my perplexity and sorrow I have heard Him say quietly, *Trust Me.* He knew that my question was not the challenge of unbelief or resentment. I have never doubted that He loves me, but I have sometimes felt like St. Teresa of Avila who, when she was dumped out of a carriage into a ditch, said, "If this is the way You treat Your friends, no wonder You have so few!" Job was not, it seems to me, a very patient man. But he never gave up his conviction that he was in God's hands. God was big enough to take whatever Job dished out.... Do not be afraid to tell Him exactly how you feel (He's already read your thoughts anyway). Don't tell the whole world. God can take it—others can't. Then listen for His answer. Six scriptural answers to the question WHY come from: 1 Peter 4:12-13; Romans 5:3-4; 2 Corinthians 12:9; John 14:31; Romans 8:17; Colossians 1:24. There is mystery, but it is not all mystery. Here are clear reasons.

Keep a Quiet Heart

Understand

THE SACRIFICE

Oh, teach me what it meaneth—
That cross uplifted high,
With One—the Man of Sorrows—
Condemned to bleed and die!
Oh, teach me what it cost Thee
To make a sinner whole;
And teach me, Savior, teach me,
The value of a soul!

Oh, teach me what it meaneth—
Thy love beyond compare,
The love that reacheth deeper
Than depths of self-despair!
Yes, teach me, till there gloweth
In this cold heart of mine
Some feeble, pale reflection
Of that pure love of Thine.

Lucy Bennett

VALUE ...

Your "April Days"

oes any soul, young in physical or in spiritual life, shrink back and say, "I would rather remain in the springtime—I do not want to reach unto the things that are before if it means all this matter of pain and dying."

To such comes the Master's voice, "Fear none of those things which thou shalt suffer" (Revelation 2:10, KJV). You are right to be glad in His April days while He gives them. Every stage of the heavenly growth in us is lovely to Him; He is the God of the daisies and the lambs and the merry child hearts!

Lilias Trotter

VALUE ...

God's Grace

O Lord, by all Thy dealings with us, whether of joy or pain, of light or darkness, let us be brought to Thee. Let us value no treatment of Thy grace simply because it makes us happy or because it makes us sad, because it gives us or denies us what we want; but may all that Thou sendest us bring us to Thee, that, knowing Thy perfectness, we may be sure in every disappointment that Thou art still loving us, and in every darkness that Thou art still enlightening us, and in every enforced idleness that Thou art still using us; yea, in every death that Thou art still giving us life, as in His death Thou didst give life to Thy Son, our Savior, Jesus Christ. Amen.

Phillips Brooks

Value

PAST LESSONS

God is the God of our yesterdays, and He allows the memory of them in order to turn the past into a ministry of spiritual culture for the future. God reminds us of the past lest we get into a shallow security in the present....

...Our yesterdays present irreparable things to us; it is true that we have lost opportunities which will never return, but God can transform this destructive anxiety into a constructive thoughtfulness for the future. Let the past sleep, but let it sleep on the bosom of Christ.

Leave the Irreparable Past in His hands, and step out into the Irresistible Future with Him.

Oswald Chambers

VALUE ...

This Ring-Round Love

Dearest, when thou desirest to buy a ring—
Sweetheart, in this obey me without fail;
Give me no diamond which is for sale—
It is too glittering, too cold a thing.
Buy me no platinum; I cannot sing
Of such a metal, precious, but too pale!
And bandits' robbing soon would end the tale.
Thy love is more than ransom for a king.
It is enough that I should have thy heart.
And when thou tak'st me, Lover, for thy bride,
Give me a ring of gold, not thick nor wide,
Pure gold like thee, God's finest work of art.
I also thought: into the Heavens new,
Where streets are gold, I might take thy ring, too.

Betty Scott Stam, "Ring: Sonnet"

VALUE ...

God's Creation

*H*eaven above is softer blue,
Earth around is sweeter green!
Something lives in every hue
Christless eyes have never seen:
Birds with gladder songs o'erflow,
Flowers with deeper beauties shine,
Since I know, as now I know,
I am His, and He is mine.

George Wade Robinson

*F*eel that I must write something tonight in praise of the God of delights.... To stand embraced by the shadows of a friendly tree with the wind tugging at your coattails and the heavens hailing your heart—to gaze and glory and to give oneself again to God, what more could a man ask?

Jim Elliot, from Shadow of the Almighty

WORK ...

And Do the Next Thing

From an old English parsonage, down by the sea
There came in the twilight a message to me;
Its quaint Saxon legend, deeply engraven,
Hath, as it seems to me, teaching from Heaven.
And on through the hours the quiet words ring
Like a low inspiration—"DO THE NEXT THING."

Many a questioning, many a fear,
Many a doubt, hath its quieting here.
Moment by moment, let down from Heaven,
Time, opportunity, guidance, are given.
Fear not tomorrows, Child of the King,
Trust them with Jesus, "DO THE NEXT THING."

Do it immediately; do it with prayer;
Do it reliantly, casting all care;
Do it with reverence, tracing His Hand
Who placed it before thee with earnest command.
Stayed on Omnipotence, safe neath His wing,
Leave all resultings, "DO THE NEXT THING."

Looking to Jesus, ever serener,

(Working or suffering) be thy demeanor,

In His dear presence, the rest of His calm,

The light of His countenance be thy psalm,

Strong in His faithfulness, praise and sing,

Then, as He beckons thee, "DO THE NEXT THING."

Author unknown

Whatever your hand finds to do,
do it with all your might.

ECCLESIASTES 9:10

WORK ...

For the Glory of God

*I*s work a necessary evil, even a curse? A Christian who spent many years in Soviet work camps, learning to know work at its most brutal, its most degrading and dehumanizing, testified that he took pride in it, did the best he could, worked to the limit of his strength each day. Why? Because he saw it as a gift from God, coming to him from the hand of God, the very will of God for him. He remembered that Jesus did not make benches and roofbeams and plow handles by means of miracles, but by means of saw, axe, and adze.

Wouldn't it make an astounding difference, not only in the quality of the work we do (in office, schoolroom, factory, kitchen, or backyard), but also in our satisfaction, even our joy, if we recognized God's gracious gift in every single task, from making a bed or bathing a baby to drawing a blueprint or selling a computer? If our children saw us doing "heartily as unto the Lord" all the work we do, they would learn true happiness. Instead of feeling that they must be allowed to do what they like, they would learn to like what they do.

Keep a Quiet Heart

Work

AND TRUST TIME WILL
BE GIVEN TO FINISH

I think I find most help in trying to look on all the interruptions and hindrances to work that one has planned out for oneself as discipline, trials sent by God to help one against getting selfish over one's work. Then one can feel that perhaps one's true work—one's work for God—consists in doing some trifling haphazard thing that has been thrown into one's day. It is not a waste of time, as one is tempted to think, it is the most important part of the work of the day—the part one can best offer to God. After such a hindrance, do not rush after the planned work; trust that the time to finish it will be given sometime, and keep a quiet heart about it.

Annie Keary

Work...
AND REJOICE

I do not know when I have had happier times in my soul, than when I have been sitting at work, with nothing before me but a candle and a white cloth, and hearing no sound but that of my own breath, with God in my soul and heaven in my eye.... I rejoice in being exactly what I am, a creature capable of loving God, and who, as long as God lives, must be happy. I get up and look for a while out of the window, and gaze at the moon and stars, the work of an Almighty hand. I think of the grandeur of the universe, and then sit down, and think myself one of the happiest beings in it.

A poor Methodist woman, eighteenth century

YEARN ...

To Be Growing Holier

*O*ld age can seem like a hot wind, whistling in from some unseen desert, withering and desiccating with a speed that takes our breath away. Wear and tear make their indelible marks on the face in the mirror which (weirdly and shockingly sometimes) becomes the face of a stranger. Fear grips us as we take note of what has gone and contemplate what is to come. The spectres of loneliness, illness, abandonment, and the serial deprivation of our powers stare back at us from the furrowed and sagging face. But God will be there. There is no need to fear the future, God is already there, and God's promise for us is, "They shall still bring forth fruit in old age" (Psalm 92:14, KJV).

...I will not be growing younger, but I want to be growing holier. When Malcolm Muggeridge returned to his cottage in Sussex after his last trip overseas he said he was going home to get ready to die (or something to that effect). He is an old man, but hear the words of one Jim Elliot who died at twenty-eight: "When it comes time to die, make sure that all you have to do is die." The only way to make sure of that is to live every day as though it were your last.

A Path Through Suffering

YEARN ...

For a Holy Rest

May He support us all the day long
until the shadows lengthen,
evening comes,
the busy world is hushed,
the fever of life is over,
and our work is done.
Then, in His mercy may He give us
A safe lodging,
A holy rest,
And peace at last.

John Henry Newman

YEARN ...

For Christ and His Glory

O Christ, He is the fountain,
The deep, sweet well of love!
The streams on earth I've tasted
More deep I'll drink above:
There to an ocean fullness
His mercy doth expand,
And glory, glory dwelleth
In Immanuel's land.

The bride eyes not her garment,
But her dear bridegroom's face;
I will not gaze at glory,
But on my King of grace:
Not at the crown He giveth,
But on His pierced hand;
The Lamb is all the glory
Of Immanuel's land.

Samuel Rutherford

Yearn

WITH JOY

I am like the butterfly just preparing to slip out of its old cocoon; panting for the life outside, but with no experience to tell it what kind of life that outside life will be. But I believe with all my heart that the apostle told the truth when he declared that, "eye hath not seen, nor ear heard, neither have entered into the heart of man the things which God hath prepared for them that love him" (1 Corinthians 2:9). And what better prospect could the soul have!

Then will be fulfilled the prayer of our Lord, "Father, I will that they also, whom thou hast given me, be with me where I am; that they may behold my glory, which thou hast given me" (John 17:24).

That glory is not the glory of dazzling light but it is the glory of unselfish love. I have had a few faint glimpses of this glory now and here, and it has been enough to ravish my heart. But there I shall see Him as He is, in all the glory of an infinite unselfishness which no heart of man has even been able to conceive; and I await the moment with joy.

Hannah Whitall Smith

YEARN ...

For Eternal Communion

His forever, only His;
Who the Lord and me shall part?
Ah, with what a rest of bliss
Christ can fill the loving heart!
Heaven and earth may fade and flee,
Firstborn light in gloom decline;
But while God and I shall be,
I am His, and He is mine.

George Wade Robinson

ACKNOWLEDGMENTS

Excerpts from *God's Guidance: A Slow and Certain Light.* © 1973, 1992, 1997 Elisabeth Elliot. Reprinted by permission of Fleming H. Revell, a division of Baker Book House Company.

Excerpts from *Keep a Quiet Heart.* © 1995 Elisabeth Elliot. Published by Servant Publications, P.O. Box 8617, Ann Arbor, Michigan 48107. Used with permission.

Excerpts from *A Lamp for My Feet.* © 1985 Elisabeth Elliot. Published by Servant Publications, P.O. Box 8617, Ann Arbor, Michigan 48107. Used with permission.

Excerpts from *The Liberty of Obedience.* © 1968 Elisabeth Elliot. Published by Servant Publications, P.O. Box 8617, Ann Arbor, Michigan 48107. Used with permission.

Excerpts from *On Asking God Why.* © 1989 Elisabeth Elliot. Reprinted by permission of Fleming H. Revell, a division of Baker Book House Company.

Excerpts from *Passion and Purity.* © 1984 Elisabeth Elliot. Reprinted by permission of Fleming H. Revell, a division of Baker Book House Company.

Excerpts from *A Path Through Suffering.* © 1990 Elisabeth Elliot. Published by Servant Publications, P.O. Box 8617, Ann Arbor, Michigan 48107. Used with permission.

Excerpts from *Quest for Love.* © Elisabeth Elliot. Reprinted by permission of Fleming H. Revell, a division of Baker Book House Company.

Excerpts from *These Strange Ashes.* © 1975 Elisabeth Elliot. Published by Servant Publications, P.O. Box 8617, Ann Arbor, Michigan 48107. Used with permission.

Excerpts from *The Elisabeth Elliot Newsletter.* © Elisabeth Elliot. Available from P.O. Box 7711, Ann Arbor, Michigan 48107.

Elisabeth Elliot has modelled courageous faith for more than forty years of public life. Her wisdom has been gleaned from her experiences as a twice-widowed wife, mother, grandmother, missionary, Bible translator, radio broadcaster, public speaker, and best-selling author. Her many books include *Keep a Quiet Heart*, *A Path Through Suffering*, and *The Savage My Kinsman*.